O₁

Creative
Real Estate Investing
Strategies And Tips

Copyright Notices

Table of Contents

Introduction

Hello fellow real estate entrepreneur my name is Omar Johnson and welcome to the book "Creative Real Estate Investing Strategies And Tips" where you will be given access to a treasure vault of creative real estate investing strategies from a real estate pro that will enable you to explode the profits in your real estate business.

My golden vault of creative real estate investing strategies are based on my actual experiences and they have enabled me to make a ton of cash in the real estate business.

My main purpose of giving these jealously guarded secrets and strategies away to you is to enlighten you so that you gain more insight and personally benefit by actually applying these tried and tested successful strategies to grow your real estate business exponentially. So without further ado let's get started!

Most Common Wholesaling Mistakes

Certain mistakes are so commonly made by new wholesalers entering in the real estate business that they are worth mentioning and highlighting. I have listed them below for you in a problem/solution format because what would be the point of highlighting the common mistakes and problems without offering relevant solutions?

Problem: You're buying in the wrong area.

Solution: Talk to your buyers, find out where they're buying, and try to find deals in those areas where buyers are active.

Problem: You're agreeing to pay too much for properties.

Solution: Lower your offers. A good rule of thumb when you are new at making offers is that if your all cash offer doesn't embarrass you at least a little it's probably too high.

Problem: You're working with the wrong real estate agents.

Solution: Find others who are more reasonable. There's never a shortage of real estate agents in any given area, and they tend to try to make themselves easy to find.

Problem: You're worrying too much about repair costs.

Solution: Let your buyer worry about this if you are uncertain. Make sure your seller understands that your offer is contingent upon certain inspections to verify repair costs. That way if you have contracted at a price that is higher than the offers you are receiving from your buyers, or that doesn't leave enough room for you to make an acceptable profit, you won't lose face by renegotiating a lower price with your seller.

Problem: You're not making offers because you don't have money.

Solution: If you're wholesaling it doesn't matter how much money you have. You will have money because you are making offers, not the other way around. Make lots of offers, you won't be using your personal funds to close on any of them. The more offers you make and the more deals you get in the middle of the sooner you will see results from your business.

Problem: You're not prescreening prospects properly.

Solution: Whether you're dealing with buyers or sellers, there will be many more who are unqualified than who are qualified. You need to spend as little time as possible talking with the former and as much time as possible talking with the latter. This is the art of prescreening. It involves asking the right questions to make a determination as quickly as possible if you are dealing with a prospect or a suspect.

Problem: You're not making enough offers.

Solution: Make lots of offers. Making offers and negotiating is where the main value comes from in a wholesaling business, and hence where you create the bulk of your profits. Generating leads to make offers on and realizing the profits you create are equally important of course, but assuming these aspects are tended to properly then the more time you spend making offers the greater your profit will be.

Problem: You don't have an organized follow up system.

Solution: Design a tickler file or similar file system to keep track of EVERYONE you talk with and follow up with them as appropriate. Most of the time you don't do business with a buyer or seller the first time you talk to them, but only after repeated contacts. So stay in touch!

Problem: Your investors are offering too low a price for you to profit.

Solution: Renegotiate your price with your seller. If they won't accept a lower price let them know you won't be able to buy the house. This becomes less of a problem the better you get at everything.

Problem: You're not getting any offers because the house is in a war zone.

Solution: Find out if your buyers are interested at any price. Target your marketing towards landlords who buy in the war zone.

Problem: You're not getting any offers because the property is in too bad of shape.

Solution: Find out if your buyers are interested at any price. If the house is a teardown tell the seller that you won't be able to buy it, unless you can get it for a discount from lot value and have buyers who will take it. If the house is not a teardown target your marketing towards investors who like very heavy rehabs. There are some rehabbers who specialize and thrive in this niche.

Things You Must Consider When Working With Private Lenders

The beautiful thing about using private lenders for your real estate investing business is that you get to set the terms by which you borrow. But what terms will you set?

It is necessary to design a lending program that will not only offer competitive terms to your private lenders but that will also meet your business's needs. What interest rate will you offer? Will you offer monthly payments of interest or a lump sum repayment?

How long will the term of the financing be? What will be your maximum LTV ratio when purchasing properties? How will you collect and collateralize your investors' money? What documentation will you use? What sort of system will you use to keep track of all of your outstanding loans and their due dates?

A substantial amount of thought must be given to these and similar questions in order for your private lending program to be effective.

One of the primary sources of private lending capital is funds from investors' self-directed IRAs. Lenders with money in an IRA may not withdraw the money but may direct it towards chosen investments. For you as the real estate investor this means that there is some extra paperwork involved.

In order to invest with self-directed IRA funds you must work with a custodian called a Third Party Administrator to handle the money indirectly.

Conversely, the loyalty of your lenders is your greatest asset as a real estate investor. Loyal investors lead to long-term profitable business relationships.

Loyalty stems from satisfaction as well as special treatment. Making sure that your promises to your lenders are fulfilled is the first step. Whenever possible go above and beyond their expectations. This will ensure long-term loyalty from your lenders.

And don't forget to make them feel special. Extra touches like follow up calls and thank you notes go a long way towards making someone feel like a person, which will help your lenders feel even better about doing business with you.

Also, I must importantly point out to you that as a purveyor of investment opportunities one organization that you should be aware of is the Securities and Exchange Commission, or the SEC. The SEC is a federal commission that monitors the sale of securities, or investments.

There are important distinctions that you should be aware of between selling shares in a business venture and borrowing money as a mortgage secured by real estate, but the details of making sure you are in compliance with the SEC should be left to your accountant.

Just be aware that if you are doing business within a single state then your activities will be of interest to that state's version of the SEC, and if you are doing business between states then your activities will be of interest to the federal SEC. Your business team should include a good accountant and/or attorney who can see to it that all of the appropriate filing and registration requirements are satisfied.

Dealing With Title Issues

A basic real estate contract stipulates that on or before a specified date the buyer agrees to bring cash for the purchase and the seller agrees to deliver clear title to prove that they have the right to sell the property.

Although according to the contract it is the seller's responsibility to ensure salable title, you as the investor are responsible for seeing that the deal gets done, so the process of ensuring clear title is something that you want to take charge of.

All deals must be screened for title issues prior to closing and either necessary and appropriate actions must be taken to clean the title or the deal must be scrapped because of unsolvable issues.

A title issue, also called a cloud, is any recorded document or state of affairs that prevents the transaction from getting through the title policy underwriting process because of a potential claim to the property in opposition to the seller's.

Common clouds on title are liens, which can be attached to a specific property, such as a mechanic's lien, and judgments, which can be attached to a specific individual, such as a judgment for child support.

If an individual who owns property is the defendant in a lawsuit and a judgment is awarded against that individual, then the judgment will automatically be attached to any property belonging to that person.

So a property may have involuntary liens or judgments attached to it that the seller isn't even aware of. Also, if a significant amount is owed in past due taxes then this could be attached to the property as a lien.

Another type of title issue is one involving probate. If the survivors and heirs of a deceased person do not take the will through the probate process in a timely fashion, it will eventually become null and void for purposes of transferring the property and the heirs will have to pursue other means if they want to take title.

Fixes for title issues will be individual and based on the situation, but there are a few common techniques to have in your mental toolbox.

First of all, if the issue is a lien or judgment that is attached to the property, it may be possible to contact the lien holder and ask for a release of lien. Or, it may be possible to negotiate with the lien holder to accept a discounted amount to satisfy the lien.

In cases where there is an unprobated will, the usual remedy is an affidavit of heirship. This is a document that can be prepared by your title company and that requires detailed information and signatures from the survivors of the deceased, and which can be used to transfer the title of an unprobated property to the rightful heir.

And finally, in some situations nothing simple will work and you may have to bring a suit to quiet title, which can fix some problems but involves a court action. You should have an attorney advise you if or when this becomes necessary.

Realize that title issues unsolvable by most buyers can be a reason for a seller to become motivated. Being able to fix problems that others don't know how to deal with can be a major source of profit in your real estate business. If you can recognize and capitalize on the hidden opportunities in title issues then you will have one more competitive advantage.

Making Money From Short Sales In A Down Market

I'm sure you heard about the real estate bubble burst you can't escape it. It's everywhere the newspapers, T.V., radio and the internet. The number one question that is being asked by the aspiring real estate investor is "How do I make money as a real estate investor in a "down" market? The answer to this question is a simple one by doing short sales.

What is a short sale?

A short sale is a sale of a mortgaged property where the lender accepts less than the balance of the loan. This happens when the loan is in default and the property is scheduled for foreclosure. Accepting a discount to sell right away can be cheaper than foreclosing.

Foreclosure is a costly process. In foreclosing on a property with a defaulted loan a lender incurs legal fees.

If the property is sold as a foreclosure it will almost certainly be for a discount.

The chances are the property may not sell right away, in which case the lender will become responsible for the maintenance, property taxes, and insurance of the property, often for months, as well as incur a real estate commission if and when it sells.

To a lender, therefore, selling a property before foreclosure, even at a discount, makes a lot of sense. Part of your job as a real estate investor is to convince them of this.

Profiting from short sales

The quickest way to use short sales to your advantage is by negotiating as low a price as possible to purchase the property from the lender and selling the property for as much as possible to an end buyer, sometimes wholesale but more commonly retail.

While it is possible in some circumstances to get the minimum 30% discount from ARV (after repair value) usually necessary for selling to an investor, often lenders will not allow more than a 10% to 20% discount, meaning that your end buyer will often be someone who wants to live in the property.

Short sales the ultimate goldmine

In 2007 there were 1 trillion dollars worth of adjustable rate mortgages that adjusted. In 2008, another 1.8 trillion dollars adjusted. So there are and will be plenty of opportunities for the short sale investor to make a ton of money and at the same time help people out who can't afford their loans anymore.

Here is a typical short sale deal. A homeowner owes $95,000 on a $100,000 mortgage and is three months behind in their mortgage payment. The property is valued at $120,000. You make a short sale offer of $65,000 to the lender to pay off the loan. You've just created $55,000 in profit for yourself ($120,000 market value less $65,000 payoff equals $55,000 profit after short sale.) In conclusion, it's easy to see that short sales are a great way to make money in a "down" market.

Working with Sellers in Pre-Foreclosure

In the current real estate market one of the most common reasons for a seller to be motivated enough to work with an investor is an impending foreclosure.

If your marketing efforts supply you with a regular stream of leads (as they should), you will encounter pre-foreclosure situations on a regular basis. Therefore, being able to understand and effectively deal with these types of sellers is a useful skill.

In order to understand how to work with sellers facing foreclosure it can help to empathize by visualizing yourself in the position of a typical seller faced with a foreclosure.

Probably the foreclosure is a secondary source of stress for you; your main concern is likely to be the accident or illness or job loss that caused the financial strain, and your primary focus will be on taking care of your family.

The impending loss of your home on top of this causes you to have difficulty eating and sleeping and concentrating on normal activities. Since you have no money to pay the lender and nothing new to say to them each time they call, you are in the habit of not answering phone calls and leaving your mail unopened in piles.

To top it off you are sensitive about the issue, making you want to bury your head in the sand and not talk to anybody about it, even to someone who might be able to help you.

The opportunity in this situation for you as the investor is that the seller genuinely needs help, which you can genuinely provide, so if you can get past their defenses they will probably give you the house.

Your marketing to pre-foreclosure sellers should be sensitive but persistent as well as credible and professional. Direct mail, phone calls, and door-to- door visits are all possible ways to make contact.

If appropriate you should introduce yourself as a foreclosure specialist and offer your assistance with solving their problem. If you are not genuine or do not have the seller's best interest at heart they are likely to be sensitive to this.

With effective marketing and a strong introduction you will establish the trust and cooperation of your client. From that point you will move on to discuss possible solutions. The goal of the seller is usually simply debt relief.

Equity is rarely if ever an issue. Assuming the seller is incapable of catching up with the loan and is resigned to walking away from the house, there are two tools in the quick-turn real estate investor's handbag that could be appropriate, depending on the willingness of the seller:

You could take over responsibility for the house and the payments and cash the loan out at a later date, which is called subject to, or you could negotiate with the lender for a discount and cash the mortgage out immediately, which is called a short sale.

Relevant factors to the investor are whether the house could be rented for positive cash flow with the existing payment structure, and whether the retail market is strong enough to guarantee a fast sale.

One final note: if you don't currently work with pre-foreclosure sellers, look towards networking with investors who do. They can help you develop your business in that direction, or you can at least have solid referrals for the pre-foreclosure sellers you encounter.

Direct Mail Marketing for the Savvy Real Estate Investor

Of all the different media available for broadcasting your marketing message to your target audience, one of the most effective places to get in front of prospects under certain circumstances is in their own homes. Marketing by direct mail allows you to do this as well as to establish a relationship with the prospect before they even meet you.

The basic principles of direct mail are simple. Craft a marketing message that can be written in a letter or on a postcard, obtain a list of the mailing addresses of members of your target audience, and mail your marketing materials to the list. Direct mail marketing is both easy to implement and scalable, meaning that you can send just a few mailings or a very many, and your responses will be proportional.

Do be aware, however, that a certain critical number of mailings will be required to get results; the normal range for response rates to direct mail marketing is in the .5% - 5% range.

So where does a good mailing list come from? Generally it comes from a data service company that specializes in supplying this type of information. You can request just about any type of list you can imagine, but here are a few that you might consider:

- Owners of abandoned or condemned properties.

- Owners of properties with delinquent taxes.

- Owners of properties in pre-foreclosure.

- Owners of properties in probate.

- Absentee owners or landlords.

- Owners of free-and-clear properties.

- Owners of properties with expired listings.

- Owners of properties with code violations.

- Owners who live out of state

The list that you choose will be targeted according to the types of properties you want to acquire, and your marketing message will be targeted to the types of prospects you are mailing to. It should be something that speaks to and motivates the type of seller you are trying to persuade to call you, something they will identify with.

Your marketing message will include your phone number and instruct the seller to pick up the phone and call it. Make sure it is answered by a live person or you are likely to lose the interest of your prospect immediately.

The types of mailing materials you can use include postcards, letters, or anything else more creative you can think of to send through the mail. It is important to keep in mind that people often will not respond to your offer the first time they see it but will eventually respond if it keeps appearing in front of them.

Therefore repeated exposure is key to increasing response rates.

Rather than sending the same letter or postcard over and over again, you might want to create a series of sequential mailings so that the prospects on your list will receive certain mailings in a certain order. This allows your direct mail pieces to tell a story and build confidence in the mind of the prospect.

If you aren't fond of creating your own sequential letter system, I've created a proprietary ready to use sequential letter system that is designed to attract motivated sellers in any niche.

All you have to do is personalize these letters with your name or your company's name and you are off to the races. To find out more information visit:

http://www.findingthemotivatedsellers.com

If you are serious about growing your business then direct mail is something you want to be serious about implementing as one of the most effective ways to both get your marketing directly in front of your prospects and to scale your business to any size conceivable.

Using Real Estate Investor Websites to Attract Motivated Sellers and Motivated Buyers

As a real estate investor it is important that you have a website or multiple websites in your arsenal because having a website will enable and allow you to prescreen your sellers and potential buyers as well as market and promote your real estate business 24/7/365.

We're living in the information age and people are using the internet more than ever to find solutions to their problems. Especially your potential motivated seller prospects! They will be looking for solutions to their real estate problems via the internet by using popular search engines like Google, Yahoo, MSN etc.

Therefore, it makes perfect sense for you to have a fully optimized website with a powerful message up and running to attract them and also so that they can find you. Once they have arrived at your real estate investor website they should be greeted with information about your company and the many creative ways you have to offer them to solve their present real estate woes.

Your website must also contain a property information form where your motivated seller prospects can leave their contact information as well as additional information pertaining to the property they are interested in selling. The information asked on this form will allow you to instantly pre-qualify your seller before you even talk to them.

Once this form is filled out and submitted by the seller, the information contain on it should be automatically delivered to your email address. Having an automated system in place like this eliminates all the hassles and headaches associated with talking to non-motivated sellers.

You Must Also Attract Buyers!

But what about also having a website to attract motivated buyers? As a real estate investor don't make the fatal mistake of only concentrating your marketing efforts on attracting and finding sellers for your real estate business because that is only one part of the equation.

The other part of the equation that you must also concentrate on and include in your marketing arsenal is simultaneously finding motivated buyers.

You see the two go hand in hand, once you are able to find a motivated seller and come to an agreement with that seller to creatively purchase their house, you need a motivated buyer to either cash you out and take the property off your hands or make some type of monthly payment to you that will enable you to create a positive monthly cash flow from that property. Don't you agree?

In fact, it would even make perfect sense for you to have your pre-screened list of buyers already in the can before you start acquiring inventory, that way you significantly increase your chances of selling that property or profiting from it immediately.

Personally, my website to attract motivated buyers is specifically designed to attract buyers who are looking for rent to own (lease purchase) or owner financing type situations and on the information form that I ask the interested prospect to fill out on my website I ask such relevant questions as:

What's the most you can afford to pay monthly for your new home?

What's the most you can afford to put down on your home?

Asking these types of questions allow me to pre-qualify my buyers as well as separate my prospects from the suspects. As you can clearly see having a website to attract both motivated sellers and motivated buyers are essential and a must for you as a real estate investor. Presently, my company is offering a special deal on search engine optimized "already done for you" real estate investor websites, that are designed to attract and prescreen motivated sellers, motivated buyers, wholesale buyers, and private lenders of real estate. For more information visit:

http://www.realestatewebsitestogo.info

The Real Estate Investor's Guide To Deal With Anxiety

As a real estate investor being unprepared can cause anxiety as well as kill any chances you have of closing deals with motivated sellers. It's the equivalent of taking a test without studying or practicing. You will either fail or lose unnecessarily.

George Allen, one of history's greatest football coaches, said that winning can be defined as the science of being totally prepared. So how do you prepare yourself to deal with sellers?

1) Make sure your real estate education is up to par

Why go out in the world pursuing sellers if you are totally unprepared? Make sure you study and know the essentials of real estate investing.

Whether that is knowing how to fill out a simple purchase and sales agreement, executing a lease option agreement, forming a land trust for asset protection or knowing how to use and protect yourself with a CYA (Cover your assets) agreement in the event that the seller claims that they didn't fully understand what they were agreeing to is very crucial.

A thorough real estate investing education should be an important component of your arsenal if you plan on succeeding as a real estate investor. It has been often said and rightly so "if you think education is expensive try ignorance". In real estate investing making mistakes because of you not having a proper real estate investing education will cost you tens of thousands of dollars.

The bottom line is be sure of what you're doing and no matter how long you have been in the business you should continue to grow your education.

2) Understand entrance and exit strategies so that you can craft multiple offers on the spot.

You must clearly define the outcome that you want to achieve. You must always know your entrance and exit when crafting your offer to sellers. As a real estate investor you make money when you buy.

For example, when negotiating a lease option with a seller before making your offer you should know how you are going to profit in the front end as well as the backend.

3) Be prepared to listen to uncover the seller's true motivation.

Most people are prepared to talk but never are prepared to listen. How do you uncover the seller's motivation for selling if you are busy doing all the talking and not intently listening to what they have to say?

Remember as a real estate investor you are there to offer effective solutions. How can you offer effective solutions if you don't know what the seller's problems are? The bottom line is in the real estate business and as a real estate entrepreneur you make money when you master effective listening.

Effective listening enables you to make relevant offers to sellers that have a high probability of being accepted. Having said that, here is one way that you can use that will enable you to become an effective listener.

Asking the right questions then intently listening to the answer.

You must ask the seller the right questions to get them to "open up". When you get them to "open up" you build rapport which will allow you to uncover the seller's true motivation as well as understand their present situation as it relates to their property. Once the seller has revealed to you their motivation and given you a clear understanding of their situation, you are in a prime position to offer them solutions.

Finding Missing Owners of Abandoned Properties

A common source of leads for the quick turn real estate investor that exists practically everywhere is abandoned properties. There are several advantages to pursuing these types of properties that are known to investors. One is that if a property is abandoned there is a good chance that the owner is disinterested in the property and might be willing to sell it.

Another is that since the property is not actively listed for sale there is likely to be little competition from other potential buyers. If you can contact the owner you will probably be the only investor they are speaking with. Yet another is that abandoned properties are readily available in most areas.

There are, of course, a few potential drawbacks to abandoned properties as well. One of these is the trouble it takes to find the owner, which is what this section is about.

Another is that it is very common for abandoned properties to have title issues which may be troublesome or impossible to fix. And finally, since the owner is often disinterested in the property it may have severe defects that will require a thorough inspection to reveal.

However, if you design a business model to handle these requirements effectively and efficiently, abandoned properties can be an effective source of deals.

Lists of abandoned properties can best be obtained by canvassing a neighborhood street by street with a digital camera. This will provide you with the most accurate picture of the neighborhood you have chosen to work in.

You can also work with lists acquired in other ways, such as the notice of default list, published monthly, of properties with defaulted mortgages, lists of condemned properties, lists of properties with absentee owners, or lists of fire damaged properties. These types of owners can all be located using the same methods and all have a potential to result in workable deals.

There are several different basic methods available for contacting missing owners given only a property address and the owner's name (starting with just the property address the owners name can be discovered from the county appraisal district records). The most relevant factors are time and budget constraints. If you are farming a neighborhood you can leave notices on the doors of target properties on a regular interval of once or twice a month perhaps.

You can also send a piece of mail to a property with the words "do not forward, return receipt requested", which will cause the post office to return it to you with the previous occupant's forwarding address.

You can use the services of a private eye who does this sort of thing in your area, or you can do the same work the private eye would do and use a skip tracing service to find phone numbers and relative's phone numbers for the person of interest, making as many calls as you have to until you get who you're looking for.

You can also use a specialty service like www.findtheseller.com, which specializes in providing this service to real estate investors.

The best way to approach the owner when you make contact is with honesty. Tell them you are an investor interested in buying the property, and tell them how you got their number if they ask. Get the relationship off to the right start and the work of closing the deal is halfway done.

Rapport: The Real Estate Investor's Ultimate Marketing Tool

The ultimate purpose of any marketing effort is to persuade your prospects to do business with you. Gaining the trust and commitment of a prospect is a necessary step to gaining a client. In order to become a client your prospect must feel in some way connected to you or your company. This connection is a quality known as rapport.

Rapport is simply the feeling of trust, likeability, and similarity that creates a bond between people. Rapport consists of several different components. Being able to identify these components makes it possible for you to consciously build rapport in your marketing and sales efforts.

Rapport is based on similarity. The more closely you match certain components of a person's demeanor the more likely you are to develop strong rapport. One possible component of this similarity is in how people use their voice. Pitch, intonation, speed, accent, and volume are all different components of speech that can be noticed and matched to invoke similarity and thus build rapport.

Another component of rapport is the language a person uses. This includes such features as emphasis, vocabulary, dialect, and even such distinctions as whether a person is speaking primarily in visual representations ("I see what you mean"), auditory representations ("I hear what you're saying"), or kinesthetic representations ("I feel where you're coming from").

Another possible avenue of rapport building is physiology. Many features of how a person uses his or her body can be matched without the person consciously noticing, but this mirroring of physiology will have a subconscious effect on their impression of you.

These features include elements of body language such as facial expression, posture, gestures, proximity, orientation, as well as other features of physiology such as breathing, walking, and other forms of movement.

People also develop rapport based on the contents of communication, such as ideas, interests, and attitudes. If you express ideas, interests, and attitudes similar to those of another person, this can be a bridge for building rapport as well.

In addition to looking at how rapport is built, it is also important to look at the factors that inhibit or damage rapport. In particular, there are two things that will kill rapport or keep it from developing: insincerity and inconsistency.

Of the two, insincerity is more immediately dangerous, but over the long run inconsistency will kill a relationship just as surely as insincerity. This is why you must be careful to match people's speech and physiology with subtlety, and match their ideas, interests, and attitudes with honesty. If you come across as being mocking or fake your attempt to build rapport will backfire.

Any form of communication provides opportunities to build rapport, especially those that provide repeated contact. When developing your marketing message and materials, focus on how your marketing will build rapport with your prospects, ideally before you ever meet them.

Voice can be used as a channel for building rapport any time you can talk directly to your prospects, such as over the phone or in person, but it can also be used any time you are able to include recorded voice audio as part of your marketing strategy. There are a number of Internet technologies that make this feasible.

Language can be used as a channel for rapport building whether it is spoken or written. Almost all marketing materials contain some sort of language, so this is one of the most versatile tools at your disposal for building rapport. Physiology is most important when you are face to face, although components of it can and also be detected and influence rapport building over the phone. This is also relevant whenever your marketing materials contain photographs or recorded video footage of your body.

Practically all marketing conveys ideas, interests, and attitudes as well, so you should constantly be seeking ways to make these components of communication work in your favor to build rapport through your marketing.

Non-Conventional Real Estate Financing

Unquestionably real estate is a big money business. If you are a quick turn real estate entrepreneur determined to be in the game for the long haul, it should not involve your money, however. Understanding financing is an important part of playing the game of real estate well and of designing an enduring business.

The most commonly conceived mode of real estate financing is conventional. This typically means a 30 year mortgage acquired through a mortgage broker or institutional lender. This subject is mainly important for your buyers, or for you if you also work as a loan officer.

There's really no good reason you should use conventional financing yourself, with all of the tricks you should know. The exception might be if you are a portfolio investor and are refinancing your properties, or if you are purchasing commercial properties.

Generally, the best way to take out conventional financing is any way but in your own name.

Qualification is based on the borrower's income, assets, and credit profile, and requires a personal guarantee of repayment. There are much better positions you could be in as an investor. The alternative financing methods might be referred to as non-conventional. These would include the methods of raising cash traditionally used by investors, generally known as hard money and private money.

Hard money is typically intended for the acquisition of rehab properties. It has a high interest rate, a low loan to value ratio, and usually a short term balloon note of six months or a year.

Private money just means money borrowed from a private individual, and can come from a person's savings or retirement fund, according to whatever terms you negotiate.

Qualifying for these types of financing doesn't necessarily involve your credit profile or financial status, but rather the terms and quality of the deal and your relationship with the lender. To acquire them you will have to present a deal to the lender that they will feel safe investing in.

There is a third category of financing, which might be called creative financing and which consists of other types that don't fit into the previous two categories. One example is subject to financing, which is just the lingo for taking over the existing payments when you take control of a property.

You will acquire the property by deed and bring and keep the mortgage payments current, but the loan will stay in the name of the original borrower. This is basically the safest form of financing ever invented.

A second type of creative financing is seller financing, where the seller of the property carries back a mortgage. This may only be used to partially fund the transaction, perhaps as a second mortgage, or the seller may carry everything but the down payment.

And finally, some investors now teach about how to obtain and use business lines of credit for real estate investing purposes. Capital in the form of business lines of credit and business loans is readily available to all new businesses with effective leadership.

Don't consider this to be exhaustive, because new techniques of financing are always waiting to be invented. This is an area of real estate where cleverness and creativity can unlock many doors.

Loss Mitigation Alternatives (Or When is a Short Sale not Appropriate)

With historically high rates of default on home mortgages lenders are facing many more foreclosures than they have in the past. This allows for short sale investors and pre-foreclosure specialists to thrive in the current market. However, not everyone who defaults on a mortgage should be considered a candidate for a short sale.

A short sale is only one of six loss mitigation options, and playing the pre-foreclosure game successfully requires a working understanding of the other five. In this discussion we will look more closely at all of the options available to a homeowner with a defaulted mortgage so that you will be able to present a balanced picture to your client and help them make the decisions that are in their best interest.

Does working with sellers in pre-foreclosure mean you have to be a loss mitigation expert? No, but it does mean you should be familiar with the options available to your client and be able to refer them to a different specialist whenever appropriate.

The purpose of loss mitigation options is to provide an alternative to foreclosure for homeowners who have had difficulty keeping up with their payments but who may still be willing and able to stay in their homes. Generally speaking, a lender is not likely to offer loss mitigation options to the owner of an investment property. And a short sale is usually the last choice on the lender's list of options, only slightly better than an actual foreclosure.

The first loss mitigation option, in order of the lender's preference, is a repayment plan. This is where the homeowner catches up the payments and brings the loan current, perhaps by making higher than normal payments for a set period of time. The lender experiences no loss this way.

The second option is a loan modification, where the borrower and the lender agree to new loan terms that are acceptable to both, perhaps with a lower interest rate but larger balance.

Third is a forbearance, which is where the lender allows the borrower to go for a specific amount of time without making payments, perhaps adding the back payment amount onto the balance of the loan. Those three options all apply to a homeowner who is able (eventually) to pay for the house.

For the homeowner who doesn't have the means to stay in the house, the lender's preferred option is an assumption, which is where somebody else who qualifies assumes the loan and resumes payments.

Next is a deed in lieu of foreclosure, which is where a lender agrees not to foreclose but rather accepts the property by quit claim deed, which will protect the borrower's credit somewhat. And finally, the last option considered by lenders before foreclosing is a short sale.

Understand that making use of any of these alternatives requires strict qualifying by the lender. All loss mitigation alternatives require there to be a legitimate hardship on the part of the borrower.

A repayment plan, loan modification, or forbearance will require demonstration of the borrower's ability to pay, an assumption will require the assumer to qualify for the loan, and a deed in lieu or a short sale will require documentation of the borrower's inability to pay.

As a pre-foreclosure investor, only after you have informed your client of and eliminated all other options can you confidently proceed with negotiating a short sale.

Purchasing Multifamily and Commercial Properties

Although many investors who get their start in the single family realm never aspire to bigger and better things for various personal reasons, there are those for whom eventually dealing with larger properties seems like a natural progression for their business practices to take.

If you are one of these entrepreneurs, you shouldn't let a fear of the process of purchasing multifamily and commercial properties hold you back from stepping up to the new challenge when you are ready.

This is simply a different realm of investing, meaning a slightly different game to play, but one that is in many ways no more complicated or risky than the single family game, and which is definitely more rewarding in terms of the profits produced versus the time spent. With a little patience and time spent studying, the rules of the commercial real estate game are surely within your grasp.

Value, as defined in the world of commercial real estate, is based on a property's current cash flow, taking into account any deferred maintenance issues that need to be addressed.

When negotiating in this world the key principle is that you buy at wholesale price, not retail. The wholesale price is the price justified by the property's current condition, including income, expenses, deferred maintenance, and your desired cap rate.

When calculating cash flow and cap rate always remember to factor in ALL expenses: mortgage payments, including principal, interest, taxes, and insurance, vacancy, maintenance, utilities, management, and any other specific expenses related to the property. Be very thorough with your due diligence and inspections. And never base your offer on pro forma cash flow figures.

Pro forma rates are figures projected into the future. Remember that "pro forma" means "imaginary". As for the target cap rate you choose, this can be a point of negotiation but is somewhat dependent upon appreciation. The lower the appreciation, the higher the cap rate you should demand, and the higher the appreciation, the lower the cap rate you should accept.

Financing works differently in the commercial world than in the single family realm as well. The main difference is that it is the property that needs to qualify for financing, not the buyer.

This is actually a very good thing because it means that the credit history of the person or entity making the purchase is irrelevant, and that you have the safety net of having the deal scrutinized by a lender to make sure the purchase is a justifiable outlay of capital.

Another important difference is that lenders rarely fund more than seventy percent of the purchase price for these types of transactions. Therefore you should always ask the seller to carry a second mortgage for as much of the difference as possible in order to minimize your out of pocket expenses.

Finally, understand that increasing value is the name of the game with commercial properties. You should have a plan ready to implement following the purchase for how to increase the property's cash flow and thus its value by decreasing vacancy, increasing rental value, and decreasing other expenses associated with the property.

Principles of Internet Marketing for Real Estate Investors

Some things only change very slowly or not at all. The fundamental rules of the real estate game are the same now as they have been for generations.

However, there is one key factor that makes the real estate business of the 21st century different from the real estate business of the 20th century. This is, not surprisingly, the same factor that is actively revolutionizing so many aspects of the way we live and do business: the Internet.

Without an understanding of how to harness this powerful force your business is likely to become obsolete very quickly, if it even gets off the ground. If you seek a greater understanding of how Internet marketing works and how you can use it for your real estate business, the content that you are presently reading provides a good place to start.

In order to utilize Internet marketing, you must, of course, have a presence on the Internet. Therefore getting a website in place is the first step, if you don't already have one. A website can be self- designed, custom made, or bought from a specialized provider like myself who offers both motivated seller and buyer websites. For more info just visit http://www.realestatewebsitestogo.info

Whatever its source a website serves as a virtual office and gives your potential clients a place to visit and learn about you online.

A critical element for any marketing website is a page that captures contact information, including a name and email address, from your visitors. Such a page is called a squeeze page. Once your visitors enter this information it is automatically stored in a database, building up over time into a massive list of interested prospects, or hungry fish.

It does no good to capture contact info from your visitors if you do nothing with it. Your database will be integrated with an email autoresponder, which will automatically send a pre-written series of messages within a specified time frame to each new visitor who signs up.

This way each new prospect will be contacted and followed up with on a timely basis. You can use this same email list to send available property alerts and other notifications to your interested buyers.

One tactic to grow an active, interested email list is to publish a newsletter on a subject of interest to your prospects. If your newsletters are interesting and informative this will have the double effect of generating interest from your existing list members (making them more likely to open emails they receive from you) as well as encouraging them to forward your newsletters (which of course contain your website and contact info) to friends and associates, helping to stimulate referral business.

Advertising on the Internet comes in three basic forms. The first is classified advertising. Most classified advertising on the Internet is free. In addition to Internet classified sites, craigslist.org and backpage.com being the most popular, many local papers have online versions of their classifieds as well.

The second form of advertising on the Internet is pay-per-click, or PPC, advertising. Google's Adwords program is one popular PPC advertising service. With PPC advertising, your ads are displayed in various places on the Internet, including alongside search engine results whenever someone searches for terms related to your business.

For each visitor who clicks on the ad and view your site, you have to pay the advertiser a fixed price. Thus the amount you pay for advertising is directly proportional to how many visitors your site receives.

The third form of advertising on the Internet is search engine optimization, or SEO. This refers to the art and science of designing your site to receive favorable exposure from search engines, so that whenever someone does a search for keywords related to your business, your site will have a higher ranking within the search engine results.

The higher your ranking the closer you are to the top of the results, so the more likely you are to receive traffic from search engines. This traffic is free, but SEO is a rather involved process that you can accomplish either by becoming an expert yourself or by hiring one.

The Importance Of Automating Your Real Estate Business

The pattern followed by successful entrepreneurs in real estate or any industry is to begin by learning the process hands on and taking responsibility for every operation, then to automate and delegate every part of the process so that it happens with less and less help from the entrepreneur. All real estate investors wear many hats when they begin, but eventually find ways to replace their own labor and free up their time.

One element available to allow you to free your time is technology. Real estate is an information business, and a few common and inexpensive pieces of equipment and software today can allow a single person to accomplish informational feats that use to require a fully equipped office and a secretary. The technology associated with the internet, like email, websites, and autoresponders, allows for mass marketing from your PC (or Mac).

Many of the functions necessary to run a real estate business can also be provided by other business that perform these services. Think beyond the conventional real estate services: agents, appraisers, brokers, contractors. Think of list brokers that compile lists of leads for you, mailing houses that distribute your direct mail campaigns, mailbox services that receive and automatically scan and upload incoming mail, virtual closing coordinators that handle closings, and more. They all exist.

And for functions of your business that are not preexisting services provided by a company or professional, there are still at least two more possibilities: virtual assistants and freelancing. Virtual assistants can be given detailed instructions and collect pay by the hour as a vendor, not as an employee. Projects or ongoing work of almost any sort can be hired out to freelancers, who provide professional services of all sorts.

The lone entrepreneur is a myth. Even a successful one-person business will interact with people in other businesses in the types of ways mentioned above. But there are at least four ways to work with other people in your business as well.

If you have a job for somebody to do and the resources to support it you can employ someone in the traditional way, as a W-2 employee. Or you can hire someone on a contractual or commission basis as a 1099 employee (freelancers, mentioned above, would fall under this category, for example, as would commissioned salespeople).

Besides hiring employees you can work in cooperation with another person to split profits. This can be done in an independent manner by splitting profits from specific transactions, for which a joint venture agreement is useful.

It can also be done by teaming up with someone to become equity partners in some fashion, where you share control of your business. All of these arrangements can be beneficial under the right circumstances.

Perhaps the most classic ways to automate a business are by referrals and mentorship. The most successful real estate investors have put in the time and organization to develop a referral network that keeps a steady supply of deals moving towards them. This is the easiest way, over time, to keep a business going and growing. Many also follow a model of mentorship, helping other investors with information and coaching in exchange for bringing business or supplying leads.

The aim of automating your business is not just for the sake of more profits, but for the sake of your personal freedom and the success of your business. Ideally you would probably like a business that keeps working and growing long after you are ready to do something else with your energy.

The Real Estate Investor's Guide To Networking

Business is like a game where the more people you are connected to the more points you have. Being connected means that not only do you know who they are, what they do, and have the means to contact them to make a request, but also that they know who you are, what you do, and have the means to contact you to make a request.

The relationship must reflect both ways in order to be of value to you in business. The name of this game is networking. Networking is the practice of accumulating points by getting to know people and getting them to know you through direct contact and referrals. The best part about it is that it's free; all you have to do is be creative and persistent about meeting people and be skilled about making a favorable impression.

One way to network is by telephone. Generate a list of potential clients and their phone numbers, and then call and introduce yourself. Once you are acquainted give them your spiel.

Your manner should be informal but purpose oriented; you should aim to make a friend on the phone, but have a definite picture of the information you want to both impart and receive.

If you can come up with a list of individuals looking for investment properties or a list of owners of investment properties (such as absentee owners or landlords), this is a great place to practice this technique.

You can also use email and internet technology to network. The main advantages of this practice are that you can communicate with larger numbers of people simultaneously, and much of the work can be automated by designing a web page with a sign-up link and an auto responder. Many people are doing more and more business exclusively by email these days, so this form of networking is becoming more accepted all the time.

Of course there will always be the old fashioned method of networking, meeting people face-to-face. To do this you have to go to where the people you want to network with are located. If they have an office or place of business you can meet them there, or you can seek them out at functions designed to draw the right type of crowd.

Many localities have real estate clubs that hold regular meetings and networking events just so that people in the business can get together and get to know each other. And of course, as you meet people on a day-to-day basis and out in the field you should constantly be seeking out networking opportunities.

The most important tool for this activity is your business card, which you should have several copies of available at all times when other people might be around. And of course you should never part ways with a new acquaintance without exchanging one (or more) of yours for one of theirs.

Referral business is the reason for all forms of networking as well as the fuel that drives it. The more people you know, even non-prospects, the more chances you have to receive referrals and the more business you will have. The best way to get referrals coming to you is to give out as many as possible.

Opportunities to send referrals to people you know should be something you consciously seek out. Providing referrals to those around you is a free and highly effective way of generating good will towards yourself and establishing a favorable reputation.

As A Real Estate Investor You Must Continue Your Real Estate Education

With all things that are done intentionally, education comes first. Education is primary to your success in business, and in all circumstances there is an identifiable pattern of learning that leads from thought to action.

When experiencing something new, first you hear about it or learn of its existence. Next you learn what it is. Then you learn how it works. And finally, you practice it, which is where experiential learning begins. This section is intended to discuss education, separate from experiential learning (but a little more on that below).

Your real estate education should not be looked at as a phase you go through, but rather as an ongoing process. This is a requirement to stay in business and to excel. There are at least three very good reasons why education should be continuous and ongoing.

One is that having new information can allow you to improve the process of what you're already doing, so that you can do it better. Another is that having new information can allow you to do new things that you're not already doing, such as implementing new profit centers in your business. A third is that the world is always changing so that knowledge needs to be continually updated to be useful.

The fastest way to develop yourself educationally is to actively seek out as many sources of education as possible on a continuing basis. There are three common modes of education to be aware of that can help inform your search.

One is private education that you digest on your own, which can include books, audio recordings, video recordings, websites, and online and offline newsletters. Another is participatory education, which involves some sort of interaction with an educator, and can include seminars or boot camps, conference calls, and webcasts. Yet one more is hands on education, which can be gotten by working with others already in the business.

This could take the form of a mentorship or an apprenticeship with another investor. You could also take advantages of all the resources of a local real estate club, either online or offline, which is dedicated to helping investors further their education in all sorts of ways.

As an ongoing business activity, your education deserves management and balancing against the other ongoing activities of your business as well as all of the other demands on your time.

You should work it out however is best so as to ensure that a dedicated portion of your time and resources on a regular basis go to furthering your real estate and business education.

A final word on education from experience, or experiential learning, comes last. Education can be overrated by beginning real estate investors. While it does have a large role to play in your overall progress and success, the amount you actually learn from studying educational materials is negligible compared to the amount you learn from actually performing an action or having an experience.

Keep this in perspective if you feel paralyzed by an insufficient education.

Real Estate Marketing: Farming a Neighborhood

Among the means at your disposal for collecting leads and growing your quick turn real estate business is establishing a farm area where you do business on a regular basis. This is a technique used by many different types of professionals to assure themselves a steady supply of business.

So what are the advantages to having a farm area? Familiarity is the big one. As you stake out and cultivate your territory you will become familiar with the area, the market, what types of people live there, what types of people are buying there, what types of properties are being sold, and for how much.

This makes it easier and quicker for you to evaluate deals. Having a farm area also allows you to consistently focus your marketing, leading to repeated exposure and increased response rates. If you continually market to an area with signs, fliers, business cards, and direct mail, it will become essentially saturated with your marketing message and your response rates will soar.

There are some drawbacks to farming as well, which are fairly easily overcome. The main one could be that your focus is narrowed to the area you are farming, but if you choose your farm area well then this should really be more of a help than a hindrance, because it will mean more business for you overall.

Farming does require a large time and energy investment on the part of whoever does it, but this can either be you or it can be someone you hire on a wage or commission basis or someone you partner up with. The only real reason for concern might be if you feel uncomfortable in the neighborhood you are farming, but then you might want to work in a nicer neighborhood anyway.

There are some specific tools that are necessary to employ this technique, for you or your help. A car or similar means of transportation is at the top of the list. A digital camera is also essential, as well as a notebook with a log sheet and printed maps of the farm area.

The best use of the digital camera comes from using it in conjunction with a small dry erase board to capture information. And finally, any time you are in your neighborhood you should have a stack of business cards handy.

When you farm, you're just in the field looking for leads. Go street by street, recording and photographing anything that looks interesting to you: abandoned properties, fsbos, ongoing rehabs, and anything else that gets your attention and that might put you in touch with a motivated seller or buyer.

It's important that you be consistent about farming and about placing your marketing. The more you talk to people in the neighborhood and hand out your business cards, leave your fliers on doors, and place signs in visible locations, the more business you will have, and if you are consistent your business will be. While you are driving track your progress on the map with a highlighter, so that you will be sure to cover the entire area.

If you use farming as a tool you will enjoy the benefits of working in an area where you are familiar with the neighborhood, your customers are familiar with your marketing, and your closing officer will become familiar with you.

What To Say To Sellers The Advantages Of Using Real Estate Scripts

To ensure your success as a real estate investor you must be prepared to deal with sellers. The bottom line is you must know exactly what to say to them to get the appointment and you must know exactly what to say to them to close deals. In addition, when you are faced with objections from sellers you must have logical confident responses that will lead to the close and ultimately the deal.

The best way to prepare to deal with sellers is by using scripts. Having something to follow can be greatly beneficial for your confidence and your poise. The most common way to do this is to sketch out an outline for your situation. What are the main points you want to hit, and what do you need to cover? This is a great way to help keep your thoughts organized and a great way to eliminate fear.

Following a script also keeps you from getting "tongue tied" because you don't know what to say or forgot what you wanted to say. In short, a real estate script keeps you on the right course.

As a real estate investor you should have a set of scripts handy that cover every possible situation that you might encounter with a seller. Once you have those set of scripts you must practice, practice and practice some more because it is the key to becoming a master communicator.

A great way you can practice is by utilizing family or friends. They can pretend to be the seller and you can play your investor role of wanting to obtain their property. Your comfort level with people you know should ease your anxiety.

In addition, your repetitive rehearsal will allow you to become more confident in communicating your message and your delivery will dramatically improve and become ingrained in your sub-conscious mind. As you practice, everything will become second nature to you like reciting your ABC's.

This will allow you when you are talking on the phone or meeting with an actual seller in person to be naturally automatic in your response to questions that the seller may ask you. It will also allow you to be automatic when posing your own questions to the seller.

The following is a script of what to say to a seller who is a frustrated landlord.

Seller: Hi my name is Pete and I am responding to a letter sent to me in regards to buying my property located at 1313 Mockingbird Lane.

You: Hi Pete, my name is (insert your name here) and thanks for responding to my letter to you. Let me explain to you exactly what I do. I am a real estate investor who buys houses creatively by offering win/win solutions to property owners. I have the ability to close quickly because I don't need a bank to buy your house. This eliminates any and all hassles. Can my service be of use to you?

Seller: Yes, because I'm looking to sell my house fast.

You: If you don't mind me asking, why are you selling your house?

Seller: Not a problem. The reason why I am selling my house is because I am tired of being a landlord. It's a two-family house and the 2 tenants who are renting the place for the lack of a better word suck. So I just want to get rid of the place.

You: I understand and as a former landlord I can totally relate to your situation. Sometimes you rent to tenants who decide they don't either want to pay rent or if they pay it they decide not to pay on time which poses problems.

Seller: Exactly, plus I'm tired of making repairs to the place because it puts me in the hole.

You: Speaking of repairs how much repair costs do you think your house needs?

Seller: About $20,000

You: What do you owe on the house?

Seller: That's really a personal question.

You: I buy on average 40-50 houses a year using various methods. I'm probably the most serious buyer you have talked to yet. The bottom line is to make you any type of serious offer on your house I need to know the facts. Will this be a problem for you?

Seller: No, I owe $180,000

You: What is the appraised value of the house?

Seller: $220,000

You: Will you allow me to buy your house by taking over the payments?

Seller: Yes, as long as I am able to cash out some of my equity.

You: I don't see any problem with that. Are you ready and prepared to fill out the paperwork to get it done today.

Seller: Yes

You: Ok great! Let's set up an appointment so that I can see the house.

Real Estate Marketing Is The Business

As a real estate investor and entrepreneur you must truly understand that you are in the business of marketing first and foremost. MARKETING drives the business. Your marketing's end result should be that it produces leads and prospects to whom you would inevitably like to present offers to and get them accepted.

The bottom line is your real estate business cannot survive without you generating a steady stream of prospects for it. So therefore, the key to making money in real estate is marketing. Never forget this. You may know 100 different ways to buy houses but it doesn't mean spit if you don't have sellers in front of you to apply what you know. Make sense? Good.

Don't get me wrong your real estate education is super important but you don't have to spend all of your valuable time learning every detail of the technical strategies of creative real estate investing. Your #1 aim should be to put yourself in the position to make profits.

The way that you put yourself in the position to make profits is by crafting a message that is designed to attract motivated seller prospects and delivering that message through the right medium. This is known as the message to market match and should be the basis of your marketing attack.

Essentially, what you are trying to accomplish with your marketing is zeroing in and trying to identify the people who have problems and need to sell their real estate as a result of these problems.

You want these potential prospects to "raise their hand" so that you can continue to prescreen them, follow up and give them more information about your services and how you can help to solve their problems. As a real estate investor and entrepreneur you will make a ton of cash by being the ultimate problem solver and the ultimate marketer.

What kind of marketing message should you craft? It all depends on which motivated seller niche you intend on targeting. For example, if you were to target the frustrated landlord niche your message would specifically address the problems associated with having tenants like rental vacancy, not getting the rent on time or not receiving any rent at all, paying attorney and court cost to resolve these situations and others like damages done to the property by the tenants etc.

Rather than being general, your message must be meaningful and specific. For example, if you were to send a letter out to the executor in charge of a probate estate you wouldn't talk about problem tenants in that letter because it wouldn't be relevant to their situation.

In addition, as a marketer you must remember that when a potential prospect receives your message they're viewing or hearing it and trying to determine "What's in it for them"? So the message that you craft and deliver must completely answer that question or your response rate will be dismal.

Lastly, if you are not generating sufficient profits in your real estate business or if you want to generate more profits for your real estate business concentrate and improve on your marketing because it is the key to your success as a real estate entrepreneur.

Secrets of Using Land Trusts

If you own real estate or plan to invest in and own real estate in the future, you don't want to own that property in your own name. Why? Because if you do your ownership will be detailed in the public records and anyone can access your information making you extremely vulnerable.

For example, if someone is planning on suing you and they grab a hold of one of those ambulance chasing lawyers that work on a contingent fee basis, that lawyer before they proceed to take on the client, will check the public records to see if you own real estate. Why? Because if the public records show that you own real estate, they know the chances of them getting paid if a judgment is rendered is very high.

You become their target and potential payday by simply making the costly mistake of not concealing your ownership of real estate. Let me reveal to you their dirty little secret of how they determine if they will pursue you or not.

They sit back with a calculator and calculate how much equity you presently have in your property and if you have equity in your property, Bingo! They've hit the jackpot!

How do they find out that you have equity in your property? It's very easy. They simply get your mortgage information from the public records, run a few comps, do a quick calculation and they have what your property's worth down to the penny.

I know that this sounds alarming but it shouldn't be. In this day and age any half-brain moron can find out your information if it is in the public records with just a click of the mouse on the internet.

A Land Trust Will Protect Your Privacy and Conceal Your Ownership of Real Estate

So what is the ultimate solution to avoid this type of a scenario from ever happening to you? By putting your property in a land trust. When you put your property in a land trust, you conceal your ownership of real estate. Land trusts are the ideal weapon for building your impenetrable wall of defense against schemers, ambulance chasing lawyers or people who just want to sue you just because they know you own real estate.

What is a Land Trust? A Land Trust is an agreement whereby one party (the trustee) agrees to hold ownership of a piece of real property for the benefit of another party (the beneficiary).

The trustee holds the legal and equitable title to the property and must follow the instructions of the beneficiary who retains management, control and the right to receive profits from the property.

The bottom line is the property is no longer in your name and you still retain all of the benefits and absolute control. Perhaps you are asking yourself why on earth would someone use such an arrangement? As it turns out there are several advantages to controlling real estate without owning it. Here are some of those advantages:

Privacy of Ownership

The owner of record of a property held in trust is the trust itself. The trust agreement, which lists you as the beneficiary, is not made a matter of public record. Therefore holding a property in trust allows you to control the property without creating any public record listing you as the owner or associating you with the property in any way. This is a great thing if you don't like lawsuits.

Publicly owning real estate makes you a fabulous target for them. Think about it, if you were an attorney being hired to sue someone, would you rather take on a legitimate case where the defendant is actually guilty of wrongdoing but has no assets, or a case where the defendant didn't really do anything wrong but does have lots of assets?

Believe it or not, just having publicly recorded assets makes you a more appealing target to predators and creditors of all sorts regardless of what you actually do. Holding a property in trust will also keep the price you buy it and sell it for off of the public record, which can come in handy in certain situations.

Ease of Transfer

Transferring a property held in trust is much easier than transferring a property that you own. Beneficial interest in a trust is considered to be personal property, not real property. Therefore you can assign your beneficial interest in a trust to another party without a formal closing. The event is treated by the law as a transfer of personal property, not real estate.

Ease of control by Multiple Owners

If a property has multiple owners, those owners can place the property in a trust and assign themselves as beneficiaries. Then, only the trustee's signature will be required to execute documents relating to the property, rather than that of each of the beneficiaries.

So how are land trusts legally created? A land trust is legally created when real estate is conveyed to a trustee by means of a warranty deed or similar document. However, before you convey real estate to a trustee you must have a trust agreement in place that dictates the duties of the trustee.

The trustee will have legal title to the property but as beneficiary you can retain nearly all of the benefits of ownership including the beneficial interest in the land trust which entitles you to profit from the property and the power of direction which binds the trustee to carry out your instructions regarding the property.

The beneficiary of a land trust can be a single individual or multiple individuals as well as a legal entity such as a corporation or an LLC. The beneficiaries are in control and as such they are responsible for any financial obligations or judgments relating to the property.

A trustee is a single individual or organization who is not an independent agent and can not be held liable for following the instructions of the beneficiary. However, the trustee does hold a fiduciary responsibility to the beneficiaries and is required to act in their best interest.

Among the responsibilities of the trustee are:

- To keep accurate records relating to the trust

- Exercise reasonable care and skill in the management of the trust. And act only upon the specific written request of the beneficiaries

Since the trustee is the legal owner of the property trustworthiness is obviously an important consideration in the selection of a trustee. Reliability and availability should be factored in as well as the trustee will be required to sign any and all paperwork as the owner of the property.

You can select as trustee an individual you know well and trust such as a friend, relative or attorney or an institution such as a bank, a trust company or other corporation.

So to sum everything up a land trust is created by two documents. A trust agreement which outlines the roles and responsibilities of the beneficiaries and the trustee and a deed which conveys title to the newly created trust.

If you want to create your own land trusts I offer a home study course entitled **"How To Form and Operate Land Trusts"** that shows you step by step how to create a land trust from scratch in your particular state. This home study course contains all the documents and forms that you need. For more information visit:

http://www.createalandtrust.com

Secrets of Making Big Money In Real Estate

"Who Else Wants To Learn How To Make A Boatload Of Cash In Real Estate In A Down Economy Using Very Little Of Your Own Money?"

I know that after reading the opening headline you're probably a little skeptical? You're probably thinking "come on man, can you really make money in real estate using very little of your own money?" You're probably saying to yourself "doesn't it take money to make money?"

Trust me, I understand your skepticism, but the cold hard facts are the majority of the people who are millionaires today became rich as a result of investing and profiting from real estate. And the bottom line is a lot of those individuals started from scratch having very little, essentially going from rags to riches and realizing the American dream.

I know that when most people think about "real estate investing" they think about it and view it in the conventional way. The conventional way is this: You see a house that you like, you make an offer to the seller close to the retail price that they are asking and then you go down to the bank and "suck up" to some banker and give your arms, legs, fingernails and five pints of blood to obtain a loan to buy the house.

Once you have made your grand purchase, you have the intentions of sitting on that house for a few years hoping that it will appreciate enough in value so that you can eventually sell it for a higher price than what you paid for it.

Honestly, is this your view of real estate investing and how to make money in real estate? Do you follow this conventional wisdom? Because you know what they say about conventional wisdom, it is usually wrong!

Quick Turn Real Estate Investing Shatters Conventional Wisdom

You see the way that I invest in real estate and the way that I teach my students to invest in real estate has nothing to do with ever having to go to a bank to get a loan to buy a piece of property.

Quite frankly, that way of doing business is just plain too risky because when you take a loan from the bank, you take on recourse debt which means if you fail to pay back the loan the bank can come after you and will come after you for everything you got because you agreed to that when you signed on the dotted line for the loan.

In addition, with the way the state of the economy is presently in right now those zero down, 100% financing offers from lenders are a thing of the past and are never coming back. So what does that mean if you're looking to invest in real estate the conventional way?

It means that the bank requirements have drastically changed. Number one you must have excellent and pristine credit and number two you must have the ability to put down a substantial down payment to get financing.

In the world of creative real estate investing, I teach that writing a big check for real estate is a big no no because as soon as you write that big check to invest in some real estate you immediately put yourself at risk of losing that money entirely.

The type of creative real estate investing strategies that I successfully use and teach my students to use involves:

- Little or no risk

- Doesn't matter if your credit is good, bad, fair or ugly

- Requires very little money to get started (just a few measly bucks for binder deposits and you are in business).

- And finally you don't take on recourse debt. In fact, the type of debt you will be managing is the seller's debt or mortgage not your own.

There is very little risk in doing business this way because it involves you making money from managing non- recourse debt which simply means when you dot your I's and cross your T's and you do the business the way I teach, you will be able to consistently profit from real estate in a safe, honest and ethical way by providing creative solutions to sellers.

The bottom line is you will never have to worry about someone successfully coming after you because you won't be making promises to sellers that you can't keep.

So what is this unique and unconventional way of investing in real estate with little risk and quick profits called? It is referred to as quick turn real estate investing. Quick turn real estate investing is a method of doing business that relies of creativity, fast closing and large numbers of deals to create a steady, consistent and massive income.

Quick Turn Real Estate Investing is not about:

- Investing your own capital into properties for a return on investment.

- Borrowing money to buy properties.

- Buying properties and hoping that they go up in value like stocks so that you can benefit from appreciation gains.

- Pulling a fast one on sellers and buyers so that you profit in an unethical way.

Quick Turn Real Estate Investing is about:

- Doing deals creatively by finding solutions to sellers problems without risking your own capital or guaranteeing any loans.

- Profiting from controlling properties and participating as a principal in transactions without necessarily taking ownership or taking ownership for a short a time as is necessary to transfer the property to the end user.

- Closing lots of deals very quickly and generating massive income in a relatively short period of time.

This is why you should become a real estate investor who specializes in quickly turning real estate for fast profits!

There are many advantages to you as a quick turn real estate investor and here are a few of the more notable ones:

- With the right toolbox of techniques you can make workable offers to nearly any seller in almost any situation that will satisfy the seller's needs and allow you to make a profit. This allows you to maximize the number of deals you can do because you have a solution custom tailored to the needs of every client.

- Deals are opened and closed quickly with no long- term entanglements. You either get in and get out upfront with your profit or you profit upfront then maintain risk free control of the property for a period of time while receiving residual income from it, eventually receiving a large back-end profit when the property is finally sold to an end buyer.

- You can mold your business into an automated system that fits around your lifestyle to create passive continuing income without the risk and liabilities of owning rental properties.

- You can create a quick turn real estate investing business from scratch. Bootstrapping from your own time and energy with just a few important pieces of technology that are readily available to anyone.

- There is no need to stock inventory, rent an office or borrow money to start this business.

These are the nuts and bolts of quick turn real estate investing that can make you rich!

Here are the easy to apply creative real estate investing strategies and techniques that you will be employing as a quick turn real estate investor.

Wholesaling – This means that you get properties directly from the source, motivated sellers and sell them at wholesale prices to cash investors. This business is driven by bargains so the key is deep discounts for cash purchases. Get the property under contract assign or double close it, collect your paycheck and go on to the next one is the name of the game.

This business is driven mainly by a strong buyers list of cash investors looking for rehabs or rental properties, good negotiation and networking skills and not much else.

Retailing – This is the opposite end of the business where you are selling homes to the general public, usually after making improvements to improve the value. Buy wholesale, sell retail is the name of this game.

This end of the business requires knowledge of construction and relies heavily on marketing to maintain a large list of hungry homebuyers so that you can sell properties quickly after the rehab is done.

Options – This is a technique that allows you to profit from any property whatsoever where the seller is willing to accept some kind of a discount from retail value and you can generate buyers willing to pay a little more.

Get an option, market the property, then assign your option for a cash fee. Any property will work as long as you can make some room for yourself between the price demanded by the seller and the price offered by a buyer. Like wholesaling, this requires a minimum of business infrastructure and a strong buyers list.

Lease options – This is a strategy that is adaptable to a variety of situations. It can be a bona fide quick turn technique if you negotiate a lease option with a seller and then assign it for a cash fee, or it can bc used to build a portfolio of properties that you control but don't own and which generate residual monthly income.

In essence you are leasing the property with a right to sublease, as well as obtaining an option to purchase the property within a time frame you specify. You then offer your buyer the opportunity to lease before buying (in exchange for a healthy option fee). You make front end, residual, and back end profit.

Seller finance – This is a broad, all encompassing strategy that centers around using seller-carry financing. This can also provide a means of creating residual cash flow from individual properties as well as providing an alternate profit center through the creation of cash-flowing notes secured by real property.

Once you acquire a property with this type of financing, you can collect a cash down payment and monthly payments from your buyer, and often have the opportunity to generate even larger back end profits by negotiating a discount on the seller-carry note by the time your buyer is ready to buy.

Subject to – Acquiring a property subject to means rescuing a sinking seller by providing debt relief in the form of taking over their existing mortgage payments, but without transferring or personally guaranteeing the loan.

This is also a broad technique, with many feasible exit strategies, which allows for the creation of front end, residual, and back end profit on each deal you do. You cover the seller's payments by putting a tenant buyer in the property, thus enjoying the benefits once again of a cash down payment, residual monthly income, and a back-end profit when your end buyer cashes out the loan.

Short sales – A short sale is when a mortgage lender accepts a discount on an over-leveraged property headed for foreclosure, allowing you to negotiate a profit into the deal so that you can help the seller avoid foreclosure. The lender's loss is your gain.

Short sales require some specialized knowledge and expertise to effectively negotiate a discount from the lender, but the opportunities in this field have exploded in recent years and show no signs of abating. Once again a large and active buyers list is essential to be able to move these properties quickly once your discounted offer has been accepted by the lender.

If you would like to learn the aforementioned creative real estate investing strategies I offer a home study course entitled **"Secrets To Making Big Money In Real Estate With Little Cash and No Credit"**. For more information visit:

http://www.gettingrichinrealestate.com

Understanding The 1031 Tax Exchange

Real estate investors looking to sell an investment property and purchase a new one can greatly benefit from the Internal Revenue Code Section 1031. Section 1031 is one of the most powerful tax deferral tools currently available for taxpayers.

In short, this section allows for a tax-deferred exchange. This means that taxpayers do not have to pay income taxes when they sell an investment property and can reinvest the proceeds from that property into a like-kind or similar asset.

A 1031 Exchange comes with numerous advantages for taxpayers and paves a road of encouragement for real estate investors so that they might continue to invest. First and foremost, Section 1031 gives the taxpayer the ability to sell business, investment and income property and not pay federal income taxes on it if they replace it with a like-kind property.

According to the IRS, like-kind properties must be the same in character or nature. They can, however, be different in quality or grade. Real estate investment properties that qualify under this IRS code include rental houses, retail and commercial properties, apartment buildings, office and industrial buildings, ranches and undeveloped land.

Properties that do not qualify under a 1031 Exchange are personal residences, interests in partnerships, business inventory, and property owned by dealers.

While Section 1031 obviously presents a big perk for real estate investors, there is a disadvantage. Because the exchange reduces the basis for depreciation on the replacement property, the replacement property will then include a deferred gain that will be taxed in the future when the taxpayer sells his or her investment.

There are four types of exchanges made possible through Section 1031. First, is a simultaneous exchange. This type of exchange occurs when the taxpayer closes both properties on the same day. This is usually a back-to- back transaction with no lapse of time between the closings.

Second is a delayed exchange, also known as a "Starker Exchange." This type of transaction refers to the closing of the replacement property after the closing of the relinquished property. A delayed exchange does not take place on the same day.

The delayed exchange is mandated by strict time frames pursuant to Section 1031. Specific timelines are in place to allow the taxpayer a certain amount of time to search for a replacement property and sign a contract to purchase it.

Next is the reverse exchange also known as the title-holding exchange. This is an exchange that occurs when the replacement property has been closed on prior to the selling of the relinquished property. When entering into this type of an exchange, the intermediary will retain the replacement property's title until the taxpayer closes the relinquished property.

Lastly, is the improvement exchange which also serves as a title-holding exchange. This type of exchange refers to a situation that involves the taxpayer purchasing property and arranging improvements for it before it is actually received as the replacement property.

Since Section 1031 does not allow the taxpayer to improve the property, a mediator is employed to retain and close on the title of the replacement property until it is ready to enter as an exchange. Once the improvements are complete the liaison then passes on the title to the taxpayer.

As you can see, there are several situations applicable to Section 1031 that benefit real estate investors. To learn more about IRS Code Section 1031 and how to profit from it, contact your financial advisor or accountant.

How To Identify and Prescreen Motivated Sellers

To find motivated sellers you have to look for them in the right places. It's sort of like fishing you want to go where the fish are biting and once you have discovered where they are biting you want to have the right bait on your line so that you can hook them and reel them in.

But first you must understand the mindset and characteristics of a motivated seller and what are the reasons that make them motivated to sell in the first place? Here are a few of those characteristics:

1) They desperately need to sell due to circumstances.

2) They are looking for a quick solution to their problems.

3) They are not afforded the time or don't have the money to sell their house the traditional way.

4) You are possibly their last hope to alleviate their burden.

Let's face it a big chunk of your success as a real estate investor will be based on your ability to distinguish between the motivated seller and the non-motivated seller. The non-motivated seller you want to stay far away from because they will only waste your valuable time, frustrate you and leave you wondering if the real estate business is really for you.

You will never convince a non-motivated seller to turn into a motivated seller unless you are willing to pay retail prices for their house. So it is imperative that you quickly and efficiently screen your sellers to determine if they are motivated or not.

Some of the questions that you should ask in the screening process are the following:

Would you sell your house for what you owe on it?

If the seller answers yes to this question they are truly motivated and you should be able to get a free house by taking over the debt or almost free house with debt plus some cash given to the seller.

Would you let me buy your house by taking over the payments?

If the seller answers yes to this question they are truly motivated and you should be able to offer as a solution a lease option or some type of owner financing "subject to" deal.

I'm a real estate investor and I am in the business of making a profit so I can't pay retail prices for houses. Do you have a problem with that?

If the seller answers no to this question that they don't have a problem, they are truly motivated and after some negotiation you will be able to get their property at a substantial discount.

Are you willing to accept some creative financing terms that will allow me to purchase your house?

If the seller answers yes to this question they are truly motivated and you should be able to craft an offer and close a deal that involves some type of owner financing.

In conclusion of this section, as a real estate investor you will save yourself a lot of frustration by identifying and ascertaining whether or not your seller is truly motivated. Always remember that a motivated seller is someone that needs to sell.

Your Buyer's List: Growing Your Number One Asset

As a quick turn real estate investor the wealth of your business is not primarily in properties owned but in contacts and relationships, particularly with your most important clients, your buyers. Thus your number one asset is your buyers list, and it should be tended to like a tree that sprouts money for leaves.

There are fundamentally two types of buyers in the real estate market, known as wholesale buyers and retail buyers. Wholesale buyers arc professional buyers, or investors, who buy properties repeatedly as part of an ongoing business or profit seeking venture. A solid core of wholesale buyers is fundamental to a wholesaling business.

They will buy single family residences that need repairs or that have tenants in them, as well as multifamily and commercial properties. It takes a relatively small number of wholesale buyers to sustain a business compared to retail buyers, who are people buying homes to live in and expecting to pay at or near full retail value.

This is because retail buyers are more selective about the house they choose and because they tend to no longer be prospects after they have made a purchase. A large base of retail buyers is vital to any business that depends on retailing.

Half of cultivating your buyers list is growing it by adding new buyers. These will be attracted to you through your marketing by means of signs, ads, and the internet. You can put up signs advertising houses for sale in your farm area, and make use of newspaper and online classifieds to get them calling.

In the case of wholesale buyers you can also take the initiative to call them if you can identify a list of investors or landlords in your area of interest.

The other half of cultivating your buyers list is strengthening the ties you have with your buyers by staying in touch with them. It's not just the number of contacts you have that is important but also the relationships and reputation that you have with them.

You should be staying in touch on a regular basis by mail, phone, or email, preferably in the form of presenting new potential deals or potential homes to purchase. As you get to know your buyers and they get to know you, you will build the confidence and familiarity that leads to sales.

Obviously the more buyers you have on your list the better, and likewise the more information you have on each buyer the better as well. Naturally the best way to store and maintain all of this information is with some sort of computer database or spreadsheet software.

Information to be gotten from all buyers should definitely include contact information, including fax and email, information about the type of property they are seeking, and information about their financing.

If you have a website through which buyers can register then it can capture all of this information. It doesn't all have to be captured up front, though, but can also be gathered over time by means of regular email and telephone follow ups.

A strong buyers list isn't created overnight, but with time and persistence it will build the momentum to carry your business forward to uncanny profits.

Creative Real Estate Investing Home Study Courses Available by Author

What To Say & How To Talk To Sellers In Your Real Estate Transactions

For more info visit: http://www.whattosaytoaseller.com

The Real Estate Investor's Guide To Finding Motivated Sellers

For more info visit:
http://www.findingthemotivatedsellers.com

Secrets To Making Big Money In Real Estate With Little Cash And No Credit

For more info visit:
http://www.gettingrichinrealestate.com

How To Form And Operate Land Trusts

For more info visit: http://www.createalandtrust.com

Private Lending For Real Estate Investors

For more info visit:
http://www.privatelendingfunding.com

Create Your Own LLC & Family Limited Partnership

For more info visit: http://www.createyourownllc-flp.com

The Secrets Of Where To Find Deals For Your Real Estate Business

For more info visit:
http://wheretofindrealestatedeals.com/

Renegade Stealth Marketing For The Savvy Real Estate Entrepreneur

For more info visit:
http://renegadestealthmarketing.com/

How To Create & Grow A Killer Buyers List For Your Real Estate Business

For more info visit:
http://www.createakillerbuyerslist.com

What To Say To Buyers To Sell Houses Fast!

For more info visit: http://whattosaytobuyers.com

Real Estate Coaching

I also offer real estate coaching on the various creative real estate investing strategies as well as the marketing of your real estate business. As your coach I will:

- Help you clarify your vision and goals
- Help you establish your step-by-step game plan
- Help you establish and meet deadlines
- Help you evaluate your progress against your goals and vision

For Your Free Consultation Visit:

http://www.theultimaterealestatecoach.com

Made in the USA
Middletown, DE
12 November 2018